MACHIAVELLI ON BUSINESS

Strategies, Advice, and Words of
Wisdom on Business and Power

Edited and Introduced by
Stephen Brennan

Skyhorse Publishing

Skyhorse Publishing books may be purchased in bulk at special discounts for sales promotion, corporate gifts, fund-raising, or educational purposes. Special editions can also be created to specifications. For details, contact the Special Sales Department, Skyhorse Publishing, 307 West 36th Street, 11th Floor, New York, NY 10018 or info@skyhorsepublishing.com.

Skyhorse® and Skyhorse Publishing® are registered trademarks of Skyhorse Publishing, Inc.®, a Delaware corporation.

Visit our website at www.skyhorsepublishing.com.

10 9 8 7 6 5 4 3 2 1

Library of Congress Cataloging-in-Publication Data is available on file.

Jacket design by Jane Sheppard
Portrait of Niccolò Machiavelli by Santi di Tito

ISBN: 978-1-62873-798-1
Ebook ISBN: 978-1-62914-077-3

Printed in China

CONTENTS

MACHIAVELLI ON BUSINESS

INTRODUCTION

"*The chief business of the American people is business.*"

—*Calvin Coolidge*

Machiavelli has much to offer today's entrepreneur if we could but understand him aright. It is by no means too great a stretch to juxtapose and to compare these meditations on the *getting and keeping of power*—by this famous or infamous Renaissance Italian—to the exigencies and imperatives of the business leaders of our own time. One might even go so far as to assert that the political conditions pertaining in Machiavelli's time were in many ways not unlike our own *cut and thrust*— to say nothing of cut-throat—postmodern business climate. Then as now, the center seems to have given way. Then, Italy found herself politically fractured, divided into numerous city-states, each with its own system of governance, leadership, and interests, and each in conflict with the other; just as now, we see a multiplicity of economic powers and centers of business activity, enabled by technologies that are global in reach, whose practical effect is to put every corporation or enterprise into competition with every other throughout the world. Faced with this anarchy of discordant polities and competing interests, and with the near impossibility of their rational delineation, Machiavelli's answer was to focus instead on the elemental truths and norms of human behavior that motivated and explained the leadership and the practices of statecraft in his own time.

It is to that end and in this spirit that we here offer the canny reader *Machiavelli On Business.*

For five hundred years now, Niccolò Machiavelli has gotten a bad rap. So much so that we have come to regard one who we call *Machiavellian,* at least in common parlance, as one who is ruthless and devious, immoral and without conscience. The conqueror-despot Napoleon Bonaparte cited him frequently, the fascist Mussolini dubbed him his muse, and Stalin is said to have heavily annotated his own bedside copy of *The Prince.* For half a millennium Machiavelli's writings are said to have inspired all manner of political atrocities; power grabs; and oppressions, and their analysis, famously, a parlor game for tyrants.

In his own lifetime Machiavelli was pretty much unknown—except in Italy where he had some small fame as a very funny playwright—and it was not until a regime change in his hometown of Florence forced him into retirement (he had served as a diplomat and as Secretary to the Chancery of the Republic of that city) that he even began to pen the great works of political philosophy—*The Prince* and the *Discourses on Livy*—by which we best know him today. Indeed, neither of these masterworks was even printed in his lifetime. But when they were finally published in 1532—oh boy, look out!—then everybody piled on. The church fathers, hiking their skirts, shrilled "Antichrist!" and banned his books. In both France and in the German states, then convulsed by religious reformation and bloody counter reformation, he was widely excoriated: one side condemning him as an atheist and virulent anticleric, the other denouncing him as the faithful son of a corrupt ecclesiastical hierarchy. At the same time, the newly Protestant Elizabethan English attacked his Catholicism and hypocritically (Elizabeth herself was a practiced *Machiavellian* if ever there was one) deplored his wickedness. Even Shakespeare, getting in on the act, coined the phrase "murderous Machiavel." One Tudor Court wag went so far as to suggest that the Devil had taken the handle "Old Nick" in a kind of homage to the name Niccolò.

But all this high-moral dudgeon and outraged disapprobation has only served to obscure the real meaning and intention of Machiavelli's work, which was to see clearly, to look humanity straight in the eye, and, drawing on his own experiences and his reading of the Classics, meditate upon those timeless and universal rules by which people manage and prosecute their affairs. Machiavelli was well aware of the difference between right and wrong, but he was not a moralist. (It is, though, a bridge way too far to say that his work promotes immorality.) His method was to take no moral position either way. Instead he put *good* and *bad* aside, and concerned himself only with expedience and with what was effective in the getting, the employing, and the keeping of power. This exercise provides much food for thought for today's businessman or woman.

I know a guy who told me this story. Seems he worked in an office with this other fella, and one day the Guy suggested to the Fella that they ought to form a little syndicate or business. They would take the money—all the small amounts—

that they would ordinarily fritter away, combine it, and buy lottery tickets together. Should lightning strike they would split their winnings. The Fella gave it to him straight: "I can't do that," he said. "I consider you a friend, I like you, but if we ever won any real money I would have to kill you. You can't expect that I would give up thousands of dollars, maybe millions, just for friendship. Business is business, after all."

Stephen Brennan
New York City, 2014

CHAPTER 1
STARTUPS

New businesses are the lifeblood of all economies, and successful startups are justly celebrated, however a large majority of new ventures ultimately fail. There are many reasons why this is so. Most often the reasons are insufficient capitalization of the enterprise in the first place or failure to identify and access its target customers.

"Nothing is of greater importance than knowing how to make the best use of a good opportunity when it is offered."

—*The Art of War*

There is no substitute for experience. A great idea is only just that, unless you have the knowledge and ability to carry it out.

"No enterprise is more likely to succeed than one concealed from the enemy until it is ripe for execution."

—*The Art of War*

Keep your powder dry, and be ready to act when the time is right.

"[I]t is unwise to ally yourself to a prince who has reputation rather than strength. To mark the mistake made by the Sidicinians in trusting to the protection of the Campanians, and by the Campanians in supposing themselves able to protect the Sidicinians, Titus Livius could not have expressed himself in apter words than by saying, that 'the Campanians rather lent their name to the Sidicinians than furnished any substantial aid towards their defense.'"

—*The Discourses*

Be careful in your choice of business alliances. A famous-name executive or a link to a celebrated brand is never sufficient. Be certain they are able to contribute to your success.

࿎$࿎

"Men intrinsically do not trust new things that they have not experienced themselves."

—*The Prince*

Getting your customers to accept your product is one key to your success in the marketplace.

~~§~~

"Let it be noted that there is no more delicate matter to take in hand, nor more dangerous to conduct, nor more doubtful in its success, than to set up as a leader in the introduction of changes."

And . . .

"He who innovates will have for his enemies all those who are well off under the existing order of things, and only lukewarm supporters in those who might be better off under the new. This lukewarm temper arises partly from the fear of adversaries who have the laws on their side, and partly from the incredulity of mankind, who will never admit the merit of anything new, until they have seen it proved by the event. The result, however, is that whenever the enemies of change make an attack, they do so with all the zeal of partisans, while the others defend themselves so feebly as to endanger both themselves and their cause."

—*The Prince*

Leadership in a new venture is always a tricky thing. Not only for all the reasons given above, but also because of the general inertia we know to be simply a fact of life. Each new product or enterprise is, in a sense, an overthrow of what has come before.

"States that rise unexpectedly, then, like all other things in nature which are born and grow rapidly, cannot maintain foundations fixed in such a way that the first storm will not overthrow them; unless, as is said, those who unexpectedly become princes are men of so much ability that they know they have to be prepared at once to hold that which fortune has thrown into their laps, and that those foundations, which others have laid before they became princes, they must lay afterwards."

—*The Prince*

Be sure of your business plan. Have sufficient capitalization at the start. Develop a strategy for lasting however long it will take for your venture or product to take hold.

CHAPTER 2

BRANDING
THE BUSINESS

Branding your enterprise consists of
a good deal more than simply settling
on a company label. No doubt you will
look to choose a name that is attractive
and that bears some real resemblance to
your product or service, but that is only
a first consideration. Be mindful also of
the myriad associations attached to and

conjured up by your choice, shrewdly opt for one that distinguishes your firm from the competition, and remember that the brand itself is of considerable importance, perhaps your most valuable, asset.

⚜ $ ⚜

"The ordinary people always judge by appearances, and the world consists chiefly of ordinary people."

—*The Prince*

Enhance attractiveness and accessibility by canny branding.

⚜ $ ⚜

"Men in general judge more by appearances than by reality. All men have eyes, but few have the gift of penetration."

—*The Prince*

What your company seems to be is often as important as what it actually is. Witness: ecologically minded oil companies, etc.

⊷$⊷

"Occasionally words must serve to veil the facts."

—*The Prince*

If you can't be good, claim you are.

⊷$⊷

"Men are so simple, and governed so absolutely by their present needs, that he who wishes to deceive will never fail in finding willing dupes."

—*The Prince*

Know your market.

CHAPTER 3

THE DEAL

At its root all business is a matter of interaction between people, the deal is the formulation of and the engine by which these reciprocalities are enacted.

❦

"Men deceive themselves more readily in generalities, but in particulars they judge truly."

—*The Discourses*

Attend to detail, and you will know where you are.

❧ $ ☙

"Deceit is fair in war. Although in all other affairs it is hateful to lie, in the operations of war it is praiseworthy and glorious. He who gets the better of his enemy by deceit, is as much to be praised as he who prevails by force."

—*The Discourses*

For our purposes here we may understand "war" as "negotiation."

❧ $ ☙

"For, besides what has been said, it should be borne in mind that the temper of the multitude is fickle, and that while it is easy to persuade them of a thing, it is hard to fix them in that persuasion. Wherefore, matters should be so ordered that when men do not believe of

their own accord, they may be compelled to
believe."

—*The Prince*

*It's all about closing. In making the sale
or coming to a deal, it is not enough to get
your client or customer to want to do as
you propose. You have to get them to sign
on the dotted line.*

"On occasion it is wise to feign folly."

—*The Discourses*

Likewise . . .

"When an enemy makes what seems like a grave
blunder, one should always suspect some deceit
to lurk behind."

—*The Discourses*

Sometimes it is useful in negotiation to get your opposite to believe that he or she has some advantage or is putting one over on you. But don't you be the one who is fooled.

❧$❧

"The way in which we live, as opposed to the way in which we ought to live, are things so wide apart, that he who quits the one in favor of the other is more likely to destroy than to save himself; since any one who would act up to a perfect standard of goodness in everything, must be ruined among so many who are not good."

—*The Prince*

Tailor your negotiation to suit what you know about the person across the table from you.

❧$❧

"There is no disgrace in not observing promises wrung from you by force; for promises thus extorted will always be broken as soon as the pressure under which they were made is withdrawn."

—*The Discourses*

As this is an almost-universal human trait or truth, remember it goes for the other guy as well as for yourself.

৯৩ $ ৩৯

"The promise given was a necessity of the past: the word broken is a necessity of the present."

—*The Prince*

Conditions change; things happen. Therefore . . .

"A prudent ruler ought not to keep faith when by doing so it would be against his interest, and when the reasons which made him bind himself no longer exist. If men were all good, this precept would not be a good one; but as men are bad, and would not keep their faith with you, so you are not bound to keep faith with them."

—*The Prince*

Thus the best deal or arrangement is one that benefits all parties.

"Vitelli remained suspicious, the murder of his brother had taught him that you cannot trust a prince that you have previously attacked."

—*How Valentino Killed His Enemies*

What is the history of your relationship with the person or firm with which you intend to deal?

"People, deceived by a false promise of advantage, often desire that which would be their ruin; large hopes and brave promises easily move them."

—*The Discourses*

Understand that it is often useful to nurse along or encourage your opposite's delusions.

⚜

"What one does of necessity, should seem to be done by choice. In all their actions, even in those which are matters of necessity rather than choice, prudent men will endeavor so to conduct themselves as to conciliate goodwill. This species of prudence was well exercised by the Roman senate when they resolved to grant pay from the public purse to soldiers on active service, who, before, had served at their own charges. For perceiving that under the old system they could maintain no war of any duration, and, consequently, could not undertake a siege or lead an army to any distance from home, and finding it necessary to be able to do both, they decided on granting the pay I have spoken of. But this, which they could not help doing, they did in such a way as to earn the thanks of the people, by whom the concession was so well received that all Rome was intoxicated with delight. For it seemed to them a boon beyond any they could have ventured to hope for, or have dreamed of demanding. And although the tribunes sought to make light of the benefit, by showing the people that their burdens would be increased rather than diminished by it, since taxes would have to be imposed out of which the soldier's stipend might be paid, they could not persuade them to regard the measure otherwise than with gratitude; which was further increased by the manner in which the senate distributed the taxes, imposing on the nobles all the heavier and greater, and those which had to be paid first."

—*The Discourses*

There's no harm in appearing to be generous and open handed in your dealings, particularly when you know that you really have no choice in the matter.

⌘

"To abstain from threats and injurious language, is one of the wisest precautions a man can take. Abuse and menace take nothing from the strength of your adversary; instead they only make him more cautious, and inflame his hatred against you, and lead him to consider more diligently how he may cause you hurt."

—*The Discourses*

You may force a deal, but you should not appear to do so. And gratuitous abuse is almost never helpful.

⌘

"In what leagues and alliances may we trust? Since leagues and alliances are every day entered into by one prince with another, or by one republic with another, and as conventions and treaties are concluded in like manner between princes and republics, it seems to me proper to inquire whether the faith of a republic, or that of a prince is the more stable and the safer to count on. All things considered, I am disposed to believe that in most cases they are alike, though in some they differ. Of one thing, however, I am convinced, namely, that engagements made under duress will never be observed either by prince or by republic; and that if menaced with the loss of their territories, both the one and the other will break faith with you and treat you with ingratitude. As to engagements broken off on the pretext that they have not been observed by the other side, I say nothing, since that is a matter of everyday occurrence."

—*The Discourses*

In what deals or transactions are you to have confidence? Ultimately, the best deals are not founded on friendship or personality or guile or compulsion—but rather on a shared interest.

CHAPTER 4

CLIMBING THE LADDER

A euphemism for getting ahead in the corporate or business world, in Machiavelli's time climbing the ladder referred to political advancement, but it is just as apt today in the world of commerce.

࿔࿔

"Men too often climb from one step of ambition to another, seeking first to escape injury, and

then to injure others. . . . The ambitious man
seeks at the outset to secure himself against
injury at the hands of private persons and also by
the magistrates; and by this means endeavors to
gain himself friends. These he obtains by means
honorable in appearance, either by supplying
them with money or protecting them against
the powerful. And because such conduct seems
praiseworthy, everyone is readily deceived by
it, and consequently no remedy is applied.
Pursuing these methods without hindrance,
this man presently comes to be so powerful
that private citizens begin to fear him, and the
magistrates to treat him with respect. But when
he has advanced thus far on the road to power
without encountering opposition, he has reached
a point at which it is most dangerous to cope
with him; it being dangerous to contend with a
disorder which has already made progress in a
city. Nevertheless, when he has brought things
to this pass, you must either endeavor to crush
him, at the risk of immediate ruin, or else you
incur inevitable slavery by letting him alone.

For when it has come to this that the citizens and even the magistrates fear to offend him and his friends, little further effort will afterwards be needed to enable him to proscribe and ruin whom he pleases.

A republic ought, therefore, to provide by its ordinances that none of its citizens shall, under color of doing good, have it in their power to do evil, but shall be suffered to acquire such influence only as may aid and not injure freedom."

—*The Discourses*

Of course you don't want to stifle ambition within your company; you want to encourage it. But you must take care that this inevitable competition does no harm to your enterprise.

❧ $ ❧

"Whence we may draw the general axiom, which never or rarely errs, that he who is the cause of another's greatness is himself undone, since he must work either by deceit or force, each of which excites distrust in the person raised to power."

—*The Prince*

When acting in sync or combination with a colleague, be sure that your own aims, interests, and advancement are not neglected.

⋘❦⋙

"How perilous a thing it is to put one's self at the head of changes whereby many are affected, how difficult to guide and bring them to perfection, and when perfected to maintain them. What desperate dangers are incurred by the citizens of a republic or by the counselors of a prince in being the first to promote some grave and important measure, when the whole responsibility attending it rests with them. For as men judge of things by their results, any evil which ensues from such measures will be imputed to their author. And although if good ensue he will be applauded, nevertheless in matters of this kind, what a man may gain is as nothing to what he may lose . . .

When I consider in what way this danger may best be escaped, I find no other remedy to recommend than that in giving advice you proceed discreetly, not identifying yourself in a special manner with the measure you would see carried out, but offering your opinion without heat, and supporting it temperately and modestly, so that if the prince or city follow it, they shall do so of their own good-will, and not seem to be dragged into it by your importunity. When you act thus, neither prince nor people can reasonably bear you a grudge in respect of the advice given by you. For your danger lies in many having opposed you, who afterwards, should your advice prove hurtful, combine to ruin you. And although in taking this course you fall short of the glory which is earned by him who stands alone against many in urging some measure which succeeds, you have nevertheless two advantages to make up for it: first, that you escape danger; and second, that when you have temperately stated your views, and when, in consequence of opposition, your advice has not been taken, should other counsels prevail and mischief come of them, your credit will be vastly enhanced. And although credit gained at the cost of misfortune to your prince or city cannot be matter of rejoicing, still it is something to be taken into account."

—*The Discourses*

Not exactly a heroic call to arms, but in statecraft as in business, raw courage is sometimes an overrated virtue.

❧$☙

"Men, who walk almost always in paths beaten by others, and who follow by imitation their deeds, are yet unable to keep entirely to the ways of, or attain to the power of those they imitate. A wise man ought always to follow the paths beaten by great men, and to imitate those who have been supreme, so that if his ability does not equal theirs, at least it will savor of it. Let him act like the clever archers who, designing to hit the mark which yet appears too far distant, and knowing the limits to which the strength of their bow attains, take aim much higher than the mark, not to reach by their strength or arrow to so great a height, but to be able with the aid of so high an aim to hit the mark they wish to reach."

—*The Prince*

Know your stuff, and aim high.

"He who has relied least on fortune is established the strongest."

—*The Prince*

Don't count on luck. It's never a good bet.

"A prince may rise from a private station in two ways, neither of which can be entirely attributed to fortune or genius. These methods are when, either by some wicked or nefarious ways, one ascends to the principality, or when, by the favor of his fellow-citizens a private person becomes the prince of his country . . .

In examining their actions and lives one cannot see that they owed anything to fortune beyond opportunity, which brought them the material to mould into the form which seemed best to them. Without that opportunity, their powers of mind would have been extinguished, and without those powers the opportunity would have come in vain."

—*The Prince*

Opportunity and the readiness to take advantage of favorable circumstances are key ingredients to a successful rise.

"Those who by valorous ways become princes . . . acquire a principality with difficulty, but they keep it with ease. The difficulties they have in acquiring it rise in part from the new rules and methods that they are forced to introduce in order to establish their government and its security. And it ought to be remembered that there is nothing more difficult to take in hand, more perilous to conduct, or more uncertain in its success, than to take the lead in the introduction of a new order of things, because the innovator has for enemies all those who have done well under the old conditions, and lukewarm defenders in those who may do well under the new. This coolness arises partly from fear of the opponents, and partly from the incredulity of men, who do not readily believe in new things until they have had a long experience of them."

—*The Prince*

Take this as a warning: an alert regarding the challenges to any new order.

"As a prince cannot always help being hated by someone, he ought to make sure that he is not hated by everyone."

—*The Prince*

Choose your enemies.

CHAPTER 5

EXPANDING
THE BUSINESS

The rules for best growing your enterprise
may be compared to Machiavelli's guidelines
or best practices for the enlarging, keeping,
and ruling of new states.

"The wish to acquire is no doubt a natural and common sentiment, and when men attempt things within their power, they will always be praised rather than blamed. But when they persist in attempts that are beyond their power, mishaps and blame ensue."

—*The Prince*

Do what you are able to do. Do not attempt the impossible.

⌒§⌒

"We should never hazard our whole fortunes where we do not put forth our entire strength. . . . A significant risk is almost always incurred by those who, on the approach of an enemy, resolve to defend some place of strength, or to guard the defiles by which their country is entered. For unless room be found in this place of strength for almost all your army, the attempt to hold it will almost always prove hurtful. If you can find room, it will be right to defend your strong places; but if these be difficult of access, and you cannot there keep your entire force together, the effort to defend is mischievous."

—*The Discourses*

Don't bet the farm if you only intend to support your venture with half measures.

"When a newly acquired State has been accustomed, as I have said, to live under its own laws and in freedom, there are three methods whereby it may be held. The first is to destroy it; the second, to go and reside there in person; the third, to suffer it to live on under its own laws, subjecting it to a tribute, and entrusting its government to a few of the inhabitants who will keep the rest your friends. Such a Government, since it is the creature of the new Prince, will see that it cannot stand without his protection and support, and must therefore do all it can to maintain him; and a city accustomed to live in freedom, if it is to be preserved at all, is more easily controlled through its own citizens than in any other way."

—*The Prince*

Here are three methods by which a newly acquired company or enterprise may be best managed.

"I hold strongly to this: that it is better to be impetuous than circumspect; because fortune is a woman and if she is to be submissive it is necessary to beat and coerce her."

—*The Prince*

Despite the unfortunate metaphor, Machiavelli's message is clear—good luck is often a matter of being bold.

"I remember Cardinal Soderini's claim that among the reasons one might declare Cesare Borgia and his father the Pope to be great leaders is because they were so good at seeing an opportunity and taking it."

—*On How to Treat the Populace of Valdichiana*

Again, an almost universal law or prerequisite for success.

"A weak prince may maintain himself if he follows a strong prince, but no state will survive two weak princes in a row. . . . A prince who follows another of superior vigor, may reign on by virtue of his predecessor's merits, and reap the fruits of his labors; but if he live to a great age, or if he be followed by another who is wanting in the qualities of the first, the kingdom must necessarily decline. Conversely, when two consecutive princes are of rare excellence, we commonly find them achieving results which win for them enduring renown."

—*The Discourses*

The quality of the leadership is vital to the success or failure of the venture, in statecraft as in business.

CHAPTER 6

HUMAN RESOURCES

The term "human resource management" is twentieth-century business cant for the leadership or supervision of employees in a given organization. Machiavelli long ago recognized that if any enterprise is to flourish, the leader must first of all have an understanding of the nature, biases, and inclinations his or her subordinates.

⌘

"One can say this in general of men: they are ungrateful, disloyal, insincere and deceitful, timid of danger and avid of profit. . . . Love is a bond of obligation that these poor fools break whenever it suits them to do so; but fear holds them fast by a dread of punishment."

—*The Prince*

Carrots and sticks.

"The first opinion which one forms of a prince, and of his understanding, is by observing the men he has around him; and when they are capable and faithful he is always considered wise, because he has known how to recognize the capable and to keep them faithful. But when they are otherwise one cannot form a good opinion of him, for the prime error which he made was in choosing them."

—*The Prince*

The head of the company—indeed the of leader of any enterprise—from the Corporate CEO all the way down through the supervisors of a company's various teams and departments, may be judged by the quality of the individuals working under him or her. If the subordinates' work is good, this reflects well, not only upon the leader as a manager, but also upon his good judgment in hiring and his skill in retaining those subordinates. If, on the other hand, their work is poor, this invariably reflects badly on their chief, on his or her management, and judgment.

"But when you disarm them, you at once offend them by showing that you distrust them, either for cowardice or for want of loyalty, and either of these opinions breeds hatred against you."

— *The Prince*

Be sure your employees have the tools to accomplish whatever it is that you ask them to do.

ನಾ$ನಾ

"Men, thinking to better their condition, are always ready to change masters, and in this expectation will take up arms against any ruler; wherein they deceive themselves, and find afterwards by experience that they are worse off than before."

—*The Prince*

Do your people understand just how good a deal they have?

ನಾ$ನಾ

"Men ought to be either well treated or crushed, because they can avenge themselves of lighter injuries, while of the more serious ones they cannot; therefore any injury that has to be done to a man ought to be of such a kind that you do not stand in fear of revenge."

—*The Prince*

Treat your people well, or kick them down the stairs.

⚜ $ ⚜

"Citizens who have held a higher office should not disdain the lower. . . . This usage, however, is opposed to the ideas, the rules, and the practice which prevail at the present day, where the notion obtains that a citizen who has filled a great office should be ashamed to accept a less; and where the State itself permits him to decline it.

This course, assuming it to lend luster to individual citizens, is plainly to the disadvantage of the community, which has reason to hope more from, and to trust more to, the citizen who descends from a high office to fill a lower, than him who rises from a low office to fill a high one; for in the latter no confidence can reasonably be placed, unless he be seen to have others about him of such credit and worth that it may be hoped their wise counsels and influence will correct his inexperience."

—*The Discourses*

Experience is a quality that ought never be discounted.

꩜

"There is no better way of guarding against flattery, than to make people understand that they will not offend you by speaking the truth. On the other hand, when everyone feels free to tell you the truth, respect for you dwindles.... A wise prince should take another course: choose wise men for your advisors, and allow only them the liberty of speaking the truth to the prince, and only upon matters about which you ask, and nothing else. But should you question them about everything, listen patiently to their opinions, then form your own conclusions later."

—*The Prince*

Control the decision-making process.

❧ $ ❧

"He who becomes master of a city accustomed to freedom and does not destroy it, may expect to be destroyed by it."

—*The Prince*

Establish your own company or corporate culture.

❧ $ ❧

"You must not offend a man, and then send him to fill an important office or command."

—*The Discourses*

Show respect for your subordinates, particularly if you are counting on them to accomplish some important task.

"I say that the nobles ought to be looked at mainly in two ways: that is to say, they either shape their course in such a way as binds them entirely to your fortune, or they do not. Those who so bind themselves, and are not rapacious, ought to be honored and loved; those who do not bind themselves may be dealt with in two ways; they may fail to do this through pusillanimity and a natural want of courage, in which case you ought to make use of them, especially of those who are of good counsel; and thus, whilst in prosperity you honor them, in adversity you do not have to fear them. But when for their own ambitious ends they refuse to bind themselves, it is a token that they are giving more thought to themselves than to you, and a prince ought to guard against such, and to fear them as if they were open enemies."

—*The Prince*

Any subordinate who is, for one reason or another, unable or unwilling to follow instructions or pull together with the rest of the team must go.

⚜

"Well-ordered states always provide rewards and punishments for their citizens, and never permit good deeds to excuse bad actions. When Horatius vanquished the Curiatii he deserved the highest reward. But the subsequent killing of his sister was an awful crime and so outraged the Romans that despite his recent service to the State they brought him to trial for his life. To one looking at it carelessly, this might seem an instance of ingratitude, but he who considers the matter more closely, and examines with sounder judgment what the practices of a state should be, will instead blame the Roman people for finally acquitting Horatius than for putting him on trial. And this is because a well-ordered state never strikes a balance between the good and bad deeds of its citizens, one does not excuse or mitigate the other, but confers rewards for good actions and punishment for bad. When this distinction is observed, a city will live in freedom, but when it is neglected, it must soon come to ruin. If, when a citizen has rendered some splendid service to his country, this were to excuse any crime he might later commit, he would soon become so arrogant that no bonds could restrain him."

—*The Discourses*

Rewards and punishments are best administered consistently.

❦$❦

"The nature of man is such that people consider themselves put under an obligation as much by the benefits they confer as by those they receive."

—*The Prince*

Loyalty is a two-way street.

❦$❦

"It is unwise to pass immediately from leniency to severity, or to a haughty from a humble demeanor. Among the various devices used by Appius to aid him in maintaining his authority, this, trick of suddenly passing from one character to the other extreme, was of no small prejudice to him. For his fraud in pretending to the commons to be well disposed towards them, was skillfully managed; as were also the means he took to bring about the reappointment of his advisors. Most skilful, too, was his audacity in nominating himself contrary to the expectation of the nobles, and in proposing colleagues on whom he could depend to carry out his ends. But it was not so good an idea that, after doing all this, he should suddenly turn round, and from being the friend, reveal himself the enemy of the people; haughty instead of humane; cruel instead of kindly; and make this change so rapidly as to leave himself no shadow of excuse, but compel all to recognize the duplicity of his nature. For one who has once seemed good, should he afterwards choose, for his own ends, to become bad, ought to change by slow degrees, and as opportunity serves; so that before his altered nature strip him of old favor, he may have gained for himself an equal share of new, and thus his influence suffer no diminution. For otherwise, being at once unmasked and friendless, he is undone."

—*The Discourses*

A really able leader ought to be consistent in dealing with his staff.

The best fortress which a prince can possess is the affection of his people."

—*The Prince*

Again, the loyalty and affection of your people is key to a successful and healthy enterprise.

"Cola Montano, a learned and ambitious man, taught the Latin language to the youth of the principal families in Milan. Either out of hatred to the character and manners of the duke, or from some other cause, he constantly deprecated the condition of those who live under a bad prince; calling those glorious and happy who had the good fortune to be born and live in a republic. He endeavored to show that the most celebrated men had been produced in republics, and not reared under princes; that the former cherish virtue, while the latter destroy it; the one deriving advantage from virtuous men, while the latter naturally fear them."

—*Florentine Histories*

Look to your corporate culture.

"A prince may avoid the appearance of ingratitude by himself leading military campaigns as the early Roman emperors did and as the Turk does now; because when it is the prince himself who conquers the glory and gain are all his, whereas if he is absent the glory belongs instead to his captains, unless the prince discounts and belittles their accomplishments. And when he thus shows himself ungrateful and unjust, his loss may be considered greater than his gain. To the prince who, through indolence or from want of foresight, sends forth a captain to conduct his wars while he himself remains inactive at home, I have no advice to offer which he does not already know. But I would counsel the captain whom he sends, to follow one or other of two courses, and either quit his command at once after a victory, and place himself in the hands of his prince, while carefully abstaining from every vainglorious or ambitious act, so that the prince, being relieved from all suspicion, may be disposed to reward, or at any rate not to injure him; or else, should he think it inexpedient for him to act in this way, to take boldly the contrary course, and fearlessly to take all such measures as he thinks will secure for himself, and not for his prince, whatever he has gained; conciliating the good-will of his soldiers and fellow-citizens, forming new friendships with neighboring potentates, placing his own adherents in fortified towns, corrupting the chief officers of his army and getting rid of those whom he fails to corrupt, and by all similar means endeavoring to punish his master for the ingratitude which he looks for at his hands. These are the only two courses open; but since, as I said before, men do not know how to be wholly good or wholly bad, it will never happen that after a victory a captain will quit his army and conduct himself modestly, nor yet that he will venture to use those hardy methods which have in them some strain of greatness; and so, remaining undecided, he will be crushed while still he wavers and doubts."

—*The Discourses*

Whether you are the leader of the enterprise or simply acting on instruction, never be afraid to share credit for your successes.

"For it is the nature of men to be bound by the benefits they confer as much as by those they receive. Therefore, if everything is well considered, it will not be difficult for a wise prince to keep the loyalty of his citizens steadfast from first to last, when he does not fail to support and defend them."

—*The Prince*

If your people believe you have their backs, they will have yours.

CHAPTER 7

LEADING THE ENTERPRISE

When all is said and done, Machiavelli's *The Prince* is primarily a treatise on leadership.

"Problems arise when a prince acquires new possessions in lands having different languages, customs and laws from his own. Keeping these states requires much good fortune and diligence.

Often the best solution in this case is for the prince to go and live in this new state. . . . For when you are on the spot you see difficulties as they arise and remedies may be readily applied. But when you are at a distance problems become obvious only when it is too late for them to be remedied. Furthermore, if the prince is on the scene, his new state will not be despoiled by his officials, and his new subjects will come to know their new prince, and he them. And they will have more reason to love him if they are well disposed, and to fear him if they are not."

—*The Prince*

In this case we may regard Machiavelli's "new possessions" as analogous to a company that had been newly acquired— perhaps a competitor—at any rate an organization used to different management, with a different corporate culture and business plan. Here Machiavelli argues for a vigorous hands-on approach to running the new enterprise and the advantages of this approach.

❧$❧

"The other, surer course is to send colonies to one or two places, which will be as keys to that state, for it is necessary either to do this or else to keep there a great number of forces to secure it. A prince does not spend much on colonies, for with little or no expense he can send them out and keep them there. . . . But in maintaining armed men there in place of colonies one spends much more, having to consume on the garrison all the income from the state, so that the acquisition turns into a loss. . . . In conclusion, I say that these colonies are not costly, they are more faithful, they injure less, and the injured being poor and scattered, cannot hurt."

—*The Prince*

When you acquire a new company, if you are unable or unwilling to run the thing yourself, the best plan is to get your own people in to run it for you.

"He who wishes to be obeyed must know how to command."

—*The Prince*

The key word here is "how."

"From this arises a question: whether it is better to be loved than feared. I reply that one should like to be both one and the other; but since it is difficult to join them together, it is much safer to be feared than to be loved if you cannot be both."

—*The Prince*

Change the word "feared" to "respected" and you have it about right.

"Nevertheless, he must be cautious, and must not inspire fear for its own sake, and must proceed in a temperate manner with prudence and humanity, so that too much confidence in himself does not render him incautious."

—*The Prince*

Self-confidence is one thing; arrogance is another.

❧§❧

"No one should have the power to bring the government to a stop. . . . In the Venetian Republic, the great council distributes honors and offices. But more than once it has happened that the council, whether from ill-humor or from being badly advised, has declined to appoint successors either to the magistrates of the city or to those administering the government abroad. This gave rise to the greatest confusion and disorder; for, all of a sudden, both the city itself and the subject provinces found themselves deprived of their lawful governors; nor could any redress be had until the majority of the council were pacified or undeceived. And this disorder must have brought the city to a bad end, had not provision been made against its recurrence by certain of the wiser citizens, who, finding a fit opportunity, passed a law that no magistracy, whether within or without the city, should ever be deemed to have been vacated until it was filled up by the appointment of a successor. In this way the council was deprived of its facilities for stopping public business to the danger of the State."

—*The Discourses*

Delegate authority wisely, but give no subordinate the power to do real harm to your venture.

"Everyone sees what you seem to be, few know what you really are; and those few do not dare take a stand against the general opinion."

—*The Prince*

This is the mystique of leadership.

⚬§⚬

"It is most injurious when a lawmaker does not himself observe the law he has made."

—*The Discourses*

Fairness, or at least the appearance of fairness, is an important attribute of leadership.

⚬§⚬

"Wisdom consists in knowing how to distinguish the nature of trouble, and in choosing the lesser evil."

—*The Prince*

Enough said.

⚬§⚬

"Men often err in thinking that they can subdue pride with humility. You shall often find that

humility is not merely of no service to you, but
is even hurtful, especially when used in dealing
with insolent men, who, through envy or other
like cause, have conceived hatred against you . . .

A prince, therefore, should never stoop from
his dignity, nor should he if he would have credit
for any concession make it voluntarily, unless he
be able or believe himself able to withhold it. For
almost always when matters have come to such
a pass that you cannot give way with credit, it is
better that a thing be taken from you by force
than yielded through fear of force. For if you yield
through fear and to escape war, the chances are
that you do not escape it; since he to whom, out
of manifest cowardice, you make this concession,
will not rest content, but will endeavor to wring
further concessions from you, and making less
account of you, will only be the more kindled
against you. At the same time you will find your
friends less zealous on your behalf, since to them
you will appear either weak or cowardly. But if, as
soon as the designs of your enemy are disclosed,
you at once prepare to resist, even though your
strength be inferior to his, he will begin to think

more of you, other neighboring princes will think more; and many will be willing to assist you, on seeing you take up arms."

—*The Discourses*

Be bold, even when you are bested.

🍥💲🍥

"I would advise you against the claims of those who are determined to blacken the reputation of Piero Soderini, rather you ought to look these slanderers straight in the eye and you will see just what impels them. You will realize their aim is not the strengthening of the new government, but rather the bolstering of their own faction. Let me say again, it is not Soderini who is the enemy of this regime, rather it is the old order. Thus, it is the old order that ought to be assaulted, rather than Solerini."

—*Letter to Cardinal de' Medici*

Keep your eye on the ball, and you will discover that it is most often the intention or plan that is in error, rather than the person.

⤜§⤛

"The cleverest leaders, even the most powerful among them, are always sure to obey the laws, and are most likely to heed the judgment of others."

—Belfagor Arcidiavolo

Good judgment begets good judgment.

⤜§⤛

"Any one comparing the present with the past will soon perceive that in all cities and in all nations there prevail the same desires and passions as always have prevailed; for which reason it should be an easy matter for him who carefully examines past events, to foresee those which are about to happen, and to apply such remedies as the ancients have used in like cases;

or finding none which have been used by them, to strike out new ones, such as they might have used in similar circumstances. But these lessons being neglected or not understood, or, if understood by them, being unknown to rulers, it follows that the same disorders are common to all times."

—*The Discourses*

The past is future—very often.

❧$❧

"But above all he must refrain from seizing the property of others, because a man is quicker to forget the death of his father than the loss of his patrimony."

—*The Prince*

Don't be greedy. How does the old saw go? "Bears make money, bulls make money, but pigs get slaughtered."

"There are fewer difficulties in holding hereditary states, and those long accustomed to the family of their prince, than new ones; for it is sufficient only not to transgress the customs of his ancestors, and to deal prudently with circumstances as they arise, for a prince of average powers to maintain himself in his state, unless he be deprived of it by some extraordinary and excessive force."

—*The Discourses*

It ain't rocket science, after all.

"When cities or countries are accustomed to live under a prince, and his family is exterminated, they, being on the one hand accustomed to obey and on the other hand not having the old prince, cannot agree in making one from amongst themselves, and they do not know how to govern themselves. For this reason they are very slow to take up arms, and a prince can gain them to himself and secure them much more easily."

—*The Prince*

Divide and conquer.

"Men fighting in their own cause make good and resolute soldiers. It is remarkable how wide is the difference between an army which, having no grounds for discontent fights in its own cause, and one which, being discontented, fights to satisfy the ambition of others. . . . Thus it is easily understood why it is that mercenary troops are worthless; namely, that they have no incitement to keep them true to you beyond the pittance you pay them, which can never be a sufficient motive for such fidelity and devotion as would make them willing to die in your behalf.

But in those armies in which there exists no such attachment towards him for whom they fight as makes them devoted to his cause, there never will be valor enough to withstand an enemy if only he be a little brave. And since such attachment and devotion cannot be looked for from any save your own subjects, you must, if you would preserve your dominions, arm the natives of your country; as we see to have been done by all those who have brought their enterprises to a successful close."

—*The Discourses*

Give your employees a stake in the success of your venture.

"There are many who think a wise prince ought, when he has the chance, to astutely foment some enmity, so that by suppressing it he will augment his greatness."

—*The Prince*

Reputation is not everything, but it is something.

"The Romans were not only less ungrateful than other republics, but were also more lenient than others in punishing the captains for the failure of their armies. For if these erred because of disobedience, they chastised them with gentleness; while if they erred through ignorance, so far from punishing, they even honored and rewarded them. And this conduct was well considered. For as they judged it of the most important, that those in command of their armies should, in all they had to do, have their minds undisturbed and free from external anxieties, they would not add further difficulty and danger to a task in itself both dangerous and difficult, lest none should ever be found to act with valor. . . . But if to all these cares, had been added the example of Roman generals crucified or otherwise put to death for having lost battles, it would have been impossible for a commander surrounded by so many causes of anxiety to have acted with vigor and decision. For which reason, and because they thought that to such persons the mere ignominy of defeat was in itself punishment enough, they would not dishearten their generals by inflicting on them any heavier penalty."

—*The Discourses*

Reward your people well for good work, and even if they do not completely succeed, commend and encourage them.

∽§∾

"A prince or republic should not delay in conferring benefits until difficult times are at hand. . . . For if they do, then the people will consider that these benefits are only the result of the difficult situation in which the prince then finds himself and will have grounds to fear that when the danger has passed, he will take back what he gave under compulsion. . . Therefore, all who hold the reins of government ought to think beforehand of the adverse times which may await them, and of what help they may then stand in need; and ought to be as open handed with their people as they would be were they suffering under some calamity. And, whoever, whether prince or republic, but prince more especially, behaves otherwise, and believes that after the event and when danger is upon him he will be able to win men over by benefits, deceives himself, and will not only fail to maintain his place, but will even precipitate his downfall."

—*The Discourses*

Reward your people for good work, but never appear to bribe them.

"All principalities are found to be governed in one of two different ways; either by a prince, with a body of servants, who assist him to govern the kingdom as ministers by his favor and permission; or by a prince and barons, who hold that dignity by antiquity of blood and not by the grace of the prince. Such barons have states and their own subjects, who recognize them as lords and hold them in natural affection. Those states that are governed by a prince and his servants hold their prince in more consideration, because in all the country there is no one who is recognized as superior to him, and if they yield obedience to another they do it as to a minister and official, and they do not bear him any particular affection."

—*The Prince*

For our purposes, the situation in this parable may be said to be analogous to the difference between a business owned and run by a single leader and his or her team, as compared to one in which there are several executives, each with his or her own, defined spheres of authority. Today's corporations may be understood as a mixture of the two, with a single executive and his team responsible for operating the business but answering to a board of directors.

⤳$⤲

"Therefore, he who wishes to secure himself in his new principality, must win friends, must overcome all obstacles either by force or fraud, must make himself beloved and feared by the people, must be followed and revered by the soldiers, must exterminate those who have power or reason to hurt him, must exchange the old order of things for a new order of his devising, must be severe and gracious, magnanimous and liberal, must destroy a disloyal soldiery and create anew, must maintain friendship with kings and princes in such a way that they help him with zeal and offend him with caution."

And . . .

"A prince who has thus established himself, who can command, and is a man of courage, is undismayed in adversity, who does not fail in other qualifications, and who, by his resolution and energy, keeps the whole people encouraged—such a one will never find himself at a loss, and it will be shown that he has laid his foundations well."

—*The Prince*

These are the virtues of a successful business leader.

CHAPTER 8

RESPONDING TO THE BUSINESS CYCLE

The expression "timing is everything" may overstate the case in regard to best modern business practices. Yet add to this the idea of being well prepared and flexible withal, as Machiavelli does, and you will find yourself well able to navigate your company through the ups and downs of any business cycle.

෴$෴

"The malice of fortune, not being yet extinguished, the old evils returned."

—*The Discourses*

Prepare yourself and your venture for difficult times, for they will come.

⟍$⟍

"Prudent men are wont to say . . . that he who would foresee what is to be, should reflect on what has been, for everything that happens in the world at any time has genuine resemblance to what happened in ancient times."

—*The Discourses*

And . . .

"For Time, driving all things before it, may bring with it evil as well as good."

—*The Prince*

Understand the past, and you will be prepared for the future.

⚘🏦⚘

"In matters of crisis, men often judge amiss . . . as anyone who has been present at their deliberations has occasion to know. For in matters of moment, unless these deliberations are guided by men of real wisdom and experience, the conclusions they arrive at are almost certain to be wrong . . . and measures not good in themselves are by a common error judged to be good, or are promoted by those who seek public favor rather than the public advantage."

—*The Discourses*

Avoid excessive groupthink, particularly where decisive action is required.

⚘🏦⚘

"Weak states are always doubtful as to their decisions; and tardy decisions are always hurtful. . . .

Where there is doubt and uncertainty as to what we may decide on doing, we know not how to suit our words to our conduct; whereas, with our minds made up, and the course we are to follow fixed, it is an easy matter to find the words to make our decisions clear. I have noticed this point the more readily, because I have often found such uncertainties hinder the public business of our own republic, to its detriment and discredit. And in all matters of difficulty, wherein courage is needed in resolving, this uncertainty will always be evident, whenever those who have to deliberate and decide are weak.

Not less mischievous than doubtful resolves are those which are tardy, especially when they have to be made in behalf of a friend. For from their lateness they help no one, and hurt all. Tardy decisions are due to want of spirit or want of strength, or to the perversity of those who have to make decisions, who being moved to carry out some selfish purpose of their own, suffer no decision to be made, but only thwart and hinder. Whereas, good citizens, even when they see the popular mind to be bent on dangerous courses, will never oppose the adoption of a fixed plan, more particularly in matters which do not brook delay."

—*The Discourses*

Indecisiveness and the failure to take timely action are the banes of any successful enterprise.

"Wisdom consists in knowing how to distinguish the nature of trouble, and in choosing the lesser evil."

—*The Prince*

Sometimes you have to make the best of what you know to be bad choices.

"The Romans recognized potential difficulties in advance and always remedied them in time.

They never let problems develop just so they could escape a war, for they knew that such wars cannot be avoided, only postponed to the advantage of others."

—*The Prince*

Don't postpone difficult choices; this rarely works in your favor.

"For one change always leaves a dovetail into which another will fit."

—*The Prince*

Think ahead.

"Since the desires of men are insatiable, nature prompting them to desire all things, and fortune permitting them to enjoy but few, there results a constant discontent in their minds, and a loathing of what they possess, prompting them to find fault with the present, praise the past, and long for the future, even though they be not moved thereto by any reasonable cause."

—*The Discourses*

So bend your employees ambitions and even their discontents to your best use.

"In order that our freewill may not be altogether extinguished, I think it may be true that fortune is the ruler of only half our actions, and that she allows the other half or a little less to be governed by us."

—*The Prince*

Take vigorous action when and where you can.

"To enjoy constant good fortune we must change with the times. . . . We see that some men act impulsively, others warily and with caution. And because, from inability to preserve the just mean, in both of these ways they overstep the true limit and they commit mistakes in one direction or the other. He, however, will make fewest mistakes, and may expect to prosper most, who, while following the course to which nature inclines him, finds, as I have said, his method of acting in accordance with the times in which he lives."

—*The Discourses*

Be prepared to move and to adjust with the times.

⨝

"Castracini was wont to say that the road to hell was easy because one always goes downward with one's eyes shut tight."

—*Life of Castruccio Castracani*

Stay alert to challenges and opportunities,
or you will likely fail in your venture.

∽ৎ$৵৹

"When a mischief has grown up, it is safer to temporize with it than to meet it with violence. As Rome grew in fame, power, and dominion, her neighbors, who at first had not apprehended the injury which this new republic might do them, began too late to see their mistake, and desiring to remedy what should have been remedied before, combined against Rome to the number of forty nations. Whereupon the Romans, resorting to a method usual with them in seasons of peril, appointed a dictator; that is, gave power to one man to decide without advice, and carry out his resolves without appeal. Which expedient, as it then enabled them to overcome the dangers by which they were threatened, so always afterwards proved most serviceable, when difficulties arose to embarrass their republic."

—*The Discourses*

In situations of longstanding difficulty, it is a good idea to give one individual the authority to decide what is to be done.

❧ $ ❧

"Weak republics are irresolute and undecided. The course they may take depends on necessity rather than on choice. Once when a terrible pestilence had broken out in Rome, it seemed to the Equians and Volscians, a fit opportunity for crushing her. The two nations, therefore, assembling a great army, attacked the Latins and Hernicians and laid waste their country. Whereupon the Latins and Hernicians were forced to make their case known to the Romans, and to ask to be defended by them. The Romans, who were themselves sorely afflicted by the pestilence, answered that they must look to their own defense, and with their own forces, since Rome was in no position to succor them. Here we recognize the prudence and magnanimity of the Roman senate, and how at all times, and in all changes of fortune, they assumed the responsibility of determining the course their country ought to take; and were not ashamed, when necessary, to decide on a course contrary to that which was usual with them, or which they had followed on some other occasion. I say this because on other occasions this same senate had forbidden these nations to defend themselves; and a less prudent assembly might have thought it lowered their credit to withdraw that prohibition. But the Roman senate always took a sound view of things, and always accepted the least hurtful course as the best. So that, although it was distasteful to them not to be able to defend their subjects, and equally distasteful—both for the reasons given, and for others which may be understood—that their subjects should take up arms in their absence, nevertheless knowing that these must have recourse to arms in any case, since the enemy was upon them, they took an honorable course in deciding that what had to be done should be done with their permission, lest men driven to disobey by necessity should come afterwards to disobey from choice. And although this may seem the course which every republic ought reasonably to follow, nevertheless weak and badly advised republics cannot make up their minds to follow it. . . .

But of all courses the worst for a weak State is to be irresolute; for then whatever it does will seem to be done under compulsion, so that if by chance it should do anything well, this will be set down to necessity and not to prudence. . . .

We find that irresolute republics, unless upon compulsion, never follow wise courses; for wherever there is room for doubt, their weakness will not permit them to come to any resolve; so that unless their doubts be overcome by some superior force which impels them forward, they remain always in suspense."

—*The Discourses*

Stay flexible.

❦ $ ❧

"When great calamities are about to befall, signs are seen to presage, and seers arise who foretell them. . . . The causes of such manifestations ought, I think, to be inquired into and explained by some one who has a knowledge, which I have not, of causes natural and supernatural. It may, however, be, as certain wise men say, that the air is filled with intelligent beings, to whom it is given to forecast future events; who warn them beforehand by these signs to prepare for what awaits them. Be this as it may, certain it is that such warnings are given, and that always after them new and strange disasters befall."

—*The Discourses*

The future is now, could we but apprehend it.

CHAPTER 9

HOSTILE TAKEOVERS

In modern business, the hostile takeover is the operation most comparable to warfare. The goal being to "capture" the other company or to avoid capture yourself, just as in war there are deceits and stratagems to be employed: feints, negotiations, and the application of force. There are winners and losers.

"War is not so to be avoided, but is only deferred to your disadvantage"

—*The Prince*

Meet all challenges squarely and at once.

"The highest quality of a captain is to be able to forestall the designs of his adversary."

—*The Discourses*

Understand your opponent.

"A prince who is attacked by an enemy much more powerful than himself, can make no greater mistake than to refuse to negotiate, especially when overtures are made to him. For however poor the terms offered may be, they are sure to contain some conditions advantageous for him who accepts them, and which he may construe as a partial success."

—*The Discourses*

Negotiate, even if only to understand what you are up against.

"A prince ought to have no other aim or thought, nor select anything else for his study, than war and its rules and discipline; for this is the sole art that belongs to him who rules, and it is of such force that it not only upholds those who are born princes, but it often enables men to rise from a private station to that rank. And, on the contrary, it is seen that when princes have thought more of ease than of arms they have lost their states. And the first cause of your losing it is to neglect this art; and what enables you to acquire a state is to be master of the art."

—*The Prince*

Master the arts that you intend to practice.

ᘓᕲ$ᕲᘐ

"When invasion is imminent, is it better to anticipate or await it? . . . The prince who has his people armed and trained for war, should always await a great and dangerous war at home, and never go forth to meet it. But that he whose subjects are unarmed, and whose country is not habituated to war, should always carry the war to as great a distance as he can from home."

—*The Discourses*

If your enterprise is the stronger you may await you opponent and fight the battle, as it were, on your own ground—or on your own terms. Should your firm be the weaker, then you must carry the battle to your enemy and fight on his terms. Only then can you hope to be able to meet the challenges which his superior resources permit him to bring to bear.

"When a newly acquired State has been accustomed to live under its own laws and in freedom, there are three methods whereby it may be held. The first is to destroy it; the second, to go and reside there in person; the third, to suffer it to live on under its own laws, subjecting it to a tribute, and entrusting its government to a few of the inhabitants who will keep the rest your friends. Such a government, since it is the creature of the new Prince, will see that it cannot stand without his protection and support, and must therefore do all it can to maintain him; and a city accustomed to live in freedom, if it is to be preserved at all, is more easily controlled through its own citizens than in any other way."

—*The Prince*

Win or lose, have a plan for how you intend to proceed once the battle is over.

"Contrary to the popular opinion, money is not the sinews of war. Since any man may begin a war at his pleasure, but cannot at his pleasure bring it to a close, a prince before he engages in any warlike enterprise ought to measure his strength and govern himself accordingly. But he must be prudent enough not to deceive himself as to his strength, which he will always do, if he measure it by money, by advantage of position, or by the goodwill of his subjects, while he is unprovided with an army of his own. These are things which may swell your strength but do not constitute it, being in themselves null and of no avail without an army on which you can depend.

Without such an army no amount of money will meet your wants, the natural strength of your country will not protect you, and the fidelity and attachment of your subjects will not endure, since it is impossible that they should continue true to you when you cannot defend them. Lakes, and mountains, and the most inaccessible strongholds, where valiant defenders are wanting, become no better than the level plain; and money, so far from being a safeguard, is more likely to leave you a prey to your enemy. I maintain, therefore, that it is not gold, as is vulgarly supposed, that is the sinews of war, but good soldiers; or while gold by itself will not gain you good soldiers, good soldiers may readily get you gold."

—*The Discourses*

It is not money, per se, that best guarantees a favorable outcome, but rather the spirit and capability of your team that is the best assurance of success. And if you are successful, the money will follow.

"That defense alone is effectual, sure and durable which depends upon yourself and your own valor."

—*Art of War*

Count on yourself, above all.

"I am firmly convinced, therefore, that to set up a republic which is to last a long time, the way to set about it is to constitute it as Sparta and Venice were constituted; to place it in a strong position, and so to fortify it that no one will dream of taking it by a sudden assault; and, on the other hand, not so large as to appear threatening to its neighbors. It should in this way be able to enjoy its form of government for a long time. For war is made on a commonwealth for two reasons: to subjugate it, and for fear of being subjugated by it."

—*The Discourses*

Have a plan for defending your business should your competitors one day threaten your markets, assets, or other interests.

"The lion cannot protect himself from traps, and the fox cannot defend himself from wolves. One must therefore be a fox to recognize traps, and a lion to frighten wolves."

—*The Prince*

It is never enough to be one thing only.

ᥫᦔ$ᦉᥫ

"He should endeavor to show in his actions greatness, courage, gravity, and fortitude; and in his private dealings with his subjects let him show that his judgments are irrevocable, and maintain himself in such reputation that no one can hope either to deceive him or to get round him. That prince is highly esteemed who conveys this impression of himself, and he who is highly esteemed is not easily conspired against; for, provided it is well known that he is an excellent man and revered by his people, he can only be attacked with difficulty."

—*The Prince*

The reputation of a leader for good judgment and strength may in itself discourage assaults against a company.

ᥫᦔ$ᦉᥫ

"The Swiss are well armed and very free."

—*The Prince*

Stay strong.

꼭$꼭

"Among other evils which being unarmed brings you, it causes you to be despised."

—*The Prince*

What, in a business sense, does it mean to be "well armed"? Answer that and you will avoid the dangers of being "disrespected."

꼭$꼭

"For the first thing he weakened the Orsini and Colonnesi parties in Rome, by gaining to himself all their gentlemen adherents, making them his gentlemen, giving them good pay, and, according to their rank, honoring them with office and command in such a way that in a few months all attachment to the factions was destroyed and turned entirely to the duke."

—*The Prince*

A blueprint for administering the new company, should you succeed in your takeover.

⦿$⦿

"Therefore any cruelty has to be executed at once, so that the less it is tasted, the less it offends; while benefits must be dispensed little by little, so that they will be savored all the more."

—*The Prince*

Do what you must do, fast or slow, sooner or later.

⦿$⦿

"If you notice human proceedings, you may observe that all who attain great power and riches, make use of either force or fraud; and what they have acquired either by deceit or violence, in order to conceal the disgraceful methods of attainment, they endeavor to sanctify with the false title of honest gains. Those who either from imprudence or want of sagacity avoid doing so, are often overwhelmed with servitude and poverty; for faithful servants are always servants, and honest men are always poor; nor do any ever escape from servitude but the bold and faithless, or from poverty, but the rapacious and fraudulent. God and nature have thrown all human fortunes into the midst of mankind; and they are thus attainable rather by rapine than by industry, by wicked actions rather than by good. Hence it is that men feed upon each other, and those who cannot defend themselves must be worried."

—*The Prince*

Play the game, or be played by it.

"Most men don't know how to be wholly good or wholly bad. When in the year 1505, Pope Julius II went to the city of Bologna to expel the family of the Bentivogli, who had been princes there for over a hundred years, it was his intention, as a part of the general design he had planned against all those lords who had usurped Church lands, to remove Giovanpagolo Baglioni, tyrant of Perugia. But coming to Perugia, with this intention of which all men knew, Julius refused wait to enter the town with a force sufficient for his protection, but instead entered it unattended by troops, even though Giovanpagolo was there with a great force of soldiers whom he had assembled for his defense. And thus, urged on by that impetuosity which stamped all this Pope's actions, and accompanied only by his body guard, he put himself into the hands of his enemy, whom he immediately arrested, leaving a governor behind to hold the town for the Church.

All prudent men who were with the Pope remarked on his recklessness, and on the gutlessness of Giovanpagolo. They simply could not understand why this tyrant had not availed himself of this opportunity for crushing Julius, and at the same time enriching himself with plunder, the Pope being attended by the whole College of Cardinals with all their luxurious trappings. It could not be supposed that he was stayed by any promptings of goodness or scruples of conscience; because in the case of Giovanpagolo, no virtuous impulse was likely to prevail, as he lived in incest with his sister, and had murdered his kinsmen to obtain the princedom.

Thus the only inference to be drawn is that men do not know how to be wholly wicked or wholly good, and in consequence shrink from extraordinary crimes. Giovanpagolo, who thought nothing of incurring the guilt of incest, or of murdering his kinsmen, could not, or more truly dared not, avail himself of an opportunity to do a deed which many would have admired; which would have won for him a deathless fame as the first to teach the prelates how little those who live and reign as they do are to be esteemed; and which would have displayed a greatness far transcending any infamy or danger that could attach to it."

—*The Discourses*

Very occasionally an otherwise injudicious or improvident action surprisingly meets with success, and it is the very unexpectedness of this impetuous stroke that leaves even the most hard-hearted and cold-blooded adversary stunned, nonplussed, and unable to respond.

"The ends justify the means."

—*The Prince*

This is most often understood to suggest that any outrage is permissible in pursuit of one's desired aim—an excuse for all manner of villainy. However there is an ethical appreciation of this epithet that asserts that the utilization of extraordinary means is only justified in situations where the ends to be achieved are for the greater good and are likewise extraordinarily compelling. In Latin the tag is: "Exitus acta probat," which was the motto on George Washington's family crest. No one believes he was a villain.

CHAPTER 10

RISK MANAGEMENT

Though the term "risk management" is a modern expression, the concept is an old one and of vital concern to anyone engaged in launching a venture, be it of a political, military, or commercial nature.

᪥$᪥

"It is necessary for a prince wishing to hold his own to know how to do wrong, and to make use of it or not, according to necessity."

—*The Prince*

Not that doing wrong is always necessary, but when it is . . .

"The gulf between how one should live and how one does live is so wide that a man who neglects what is actually done for what should be done learns the way to self-destruction rather than self-preservation."

—*The Prince*

The idealist will often fail.

"Thus it is well to seem merciful, faithful, humane, sincere, religious, and also to be so;

but you must have the mind so disposed that when it is needful to be otherwise you may be able to change to the opposite qualities. And it must be understood that a prince, and especially a new prince, cannot observe all those things which are considered good in men, being often obliged, in order to maintain the state, to act against faith, against charity, against humanity, and against religion. And, therefore, he must have a mind disposed to adapt itself according to the wind, and as the variations of fortune dictate, and, as I said before, not deviate from what is good, if possible, but be able to do evil if constrained."

—*The Prince*

Understand the times in which you live.

"He who would reform the institutions of a free state must retain at least the facade of the old ways. Whenever one takes it upon himself to reform an old mode of government, he ought, if his measures are to be well received and carried out with general approval, preserve at least the semblance of the old order; although, in truth, the new order differs altogether from that which it replaces. When this is well managed, the people accept what seems to be for what is; as they often judge more by appearance than by reality.

This tendency was recognized by the Romans at the very outset of their civil freedom, when they appointed two consuls in place of a single king, they would not permit the consuls to have more than twelve lictors, in order that the old number of the king's attendants might not be exceeded. In this way the people were contented, and had no occasion to desire the return of their kings. Like precautions should be used by all who would put an end to the old government and substitute new and free institutions. For since novelty disturbs men's minds, we should seek in the changes we make to preserve as far as possible what was, so that if the new magistrates differ from the old in number, in authority, or in the duration of their office, they shall at least retain the old names.

This, I say, should be recognized by whoever would establish a constitutional government, whether in the form of a republic or of a kingdom. But he who would create an absolute government of the kind which political writers term a tyranny, must renew everything."

Alternately . . .

"A new prince of a province of which he has taken possession ought to make everything new. When a man becomes prince, especially if his position is insecure, he will discover that the best way to preserve his new possession is to remake all the institutions of the state; that is, to create new magistracies with new names, confer new powers, employ new men, and like David when he became king, exalt the humble and depress the great. . .moreover, he must raze existing towns and build new ones, removing the inhabitants from one place to another— in short, leaving nothing as he found it. There must be neither rank, condition, honor or wealth except that which he has himself conferred. We take the example of Phillip of Macedon, father of Alexander, who by these very means, made himself King of all Greece, and of whom Justinius wrote 'that he moved men from place to place as a shepherd moves his sheep.'

"These are no doubt cruel expedients, so contrary not only to every Christian, but to every civilized code of conduct, that a moral man might well eschew them and instead go live as a private person rather than as a ruler who unleashes such cruelty and pain upon his people. But if a man finds himself in the position described above, and is determined to command a state, he must not shrink from walking this path of evil. Most men, however, not understanding how to be wholly good or wholly bad, usually choose to walk a middle path, which of all others is the most dangerous."

—*The Discourses*

Here Machiavelli appears to argue both sides, or for two different courses of action. However this not so, it is the recognition of different circumstances or situations in which the leader finds himself that governs the choices to be made.

❧ $ ❧

"To check the arrogance of a man who is growing too powerful, there is no safer method, or less open to objection, than to forestall him in those ways whereby he seeks to advance himself . . .

Men ought to look to the risks and dangers of any course which lies before them, neither should they engage in it when it is plain that the dangers outweigh the advantages, even though they be advised by others that it is the most expedient way to take.

Should they act otherwise, it will fare with them as with Tullius, who, in seeking to diminish the power of Marcus Antonius, added to it. For Antonius, who had been declared an enemy by the senate, having got together a strong force, mostly made up of veterans who had shared the fortunes of Cæsar, Tullius advised the senate to invest Octavianus with full authority, and to send him against Antonius with the consuls and the army; affirming, that so soon as those veterans who had served with Cæsar saw the face of him who was Cæsar's nephew and had assumed his name, they would rally to his side and desert Antonius, who might easily be crushed when thus left bare of support.

But the reverse of all this happened. For Antonius persuaded Octavianus to take part with him, and to throw over Tullius and the senate. And this brought about the ruin of the senate, a result which might easily have been foreseen. For remembering the influence of that great captain, who, after overthrowing all opponents, had seized on sovereign power in Rome, the senate should have turned a deaf ear to the persuasions of Tullius, nor ever have believed it possible that from Cæsar's heir, or from soldiers who had followed Cæsar, they could look for anything that consisted with the name of Freedom."

—*The Discourses*

Weigh your options well.

"Live cheerfully, and spend as little as you can."

—Niccolò Machiavelli, *the closing of his final letter to his son*